WEEKLY WR READER
EARLY LEARNING LIBRARY

LET'S READ ABOUT
Animals
CONOZCAMOS A LOS
animales

Pelicans/ Pelícanos

by/por Kathleen Pohl

Reading consultant/Consultora de lectura:
Susan Nations, M.Ed.,
author, literacy coach, consultant in literacy
development/autora, tutora de alfabetización,
consultora de desarrollo de la lectura

Please visit our web site at: www.garethstevens.com
For a free color catalog describing Weekly Reader® Early Learning Library's list
of high-quality books, call 1-877-445-5824 (USA) or 1-800-387-3178 (Canada).
Weekly Reader® Early Learning Library's fax: (414) 336-0164.

Library of Congress Cataloging-in-Publication Data

Pohl, Kathleen.
  [Pelicans. Spanish and English]
  Pelicans = Pelicanos / by/por Kathleen Pohl.
    p. cm. — (Let's read about animals = Conozcamos a los animales)
  Includes bibliographical references and index.
  ISBN-13: 978-0-8368-8008-3 (lib. bdg.)
  ISBN-13: 978-0-8368-8015-1 (softcover)
  I. Title. II. Title: Pelicanos.
  QL696.P47P6418   2006
  598.4'3—dc22   2006037575

This edition first published in 2007 by
Weekly Reader® Early Learning Library
A Member of the WRC Media Family of Companies
330 West Olive Street, Suite 100
Milwaukee, WI 53212 USA

Editor: Dorothy L. Gibbs
Art Direction: Tammy West
Cover design and page layout: Kami Strunsee
Picture research: Diane Laska-Swanke
Spanish translation: Tatiana Acosta and Guillermo Gutiérrez

Picture credits: Cover, title © Jean-Paul Ferrero/Auscape; p. 5 © François Gohier/Auscape;
p. 7 Kami Strunsee/© Weekly Reader® Early Learning Library; pp. 9, 17 © Lynn M. Stone/naturepl.com;
p. 11 © David Parer & Elizabeth Parer-Cook/Auscape; p. 13 © Tui De Roy/Auscape; p. 15 © Vincent Munier/
naturepl.com; p. 19 © Wayne Lawler/Auscape; p. 21 © Mike Langford/Auscape

Printed in the United States of America

1 2 3 4 5 6 7 8 9 10 10 09 08 07 06

Note to Educators and Parents

Reading is such an exciting adventure for young children! They are beginning to integrate their oral language skills with written language. To encourage children along the path to early literacy, books must be colorful, engaging, and interesting; they should invite the young reader to explore both the print and the pictures.

The *Let's Read About Animals* series is designed to help children read and learn about the special characteristics and behaviors of the intriguing featured animals. Each book is an informative nonfiction companion to one of the colorful and charming fiction books in the *Animal Storybooks* series.

Each book in the *Let's Read About Animals* series is specially designed to support the young reader in the reading process. The familiar topics are appealing to young children and invite them to read — and reread — again and again. The full-color photographs and enhanced text further support the student during the reading process.

In addition to serving as wonderful picture books in schools, libraries, homes, and other places where children learn to love reading, these books are specifically intended to be read within an instructional guided reading group. This small group setting allows beginning readers to work with a fluent adult model as they make meaning from the text. After children develop fluency with the text and content, the books can be read independently. Children and adults alike will find these books supportive, engaging, and fun!

— Susan Nations, M.Ed., author/literacy coach/
consultant in literacy development

Nota para los maestros y los padres

¡Leer es una aventura tan emocionante para los niños pequeños! A esta edad están comenzando a integrar su manejo del lenguaje oral con el lenguaje escrito. Para animar a los niños en el camino de la lectura incipiente, los libros deben ser coloridos, estimulantes e interesantes; deben invitar a los jóvenes lectores a explorar la letra impresa y las ilustraciones.

Conozcamos a los animales es una nueva colección diseñada para que los niños conozcan las características y comportamientos de los interesantes animales que se presentan. Cada libro es un texto informativo de no ficción que acompaña a uno de los libros de ficción en lengua inglesa de la colección *Animal Storybooks*.

Cada libro de la serie *Conozcamos a los animales* está especialmente diseñado para ayudar a los jóvenes lectores en el proceso de lectura. Los temas familiares llaman la atención de los niños y los invitan a leer una y otra vez. Las fotografías a todo color y el tamaño de la letra ayudan aún más al estudiante en el proceso de lectura.

Además de servir como maravillosos libros ilustrados en escuelas, bibliotecas, hogares y otros lugares donde los niños aprenden a amar la lectura, estos libros han sido especialmente concebidos para ser leídos en un grupo de lectura guiada. Este contexto permite que los lectores incipientes trabajen con un adulto que domina la lectura mientras van determinando el significado del texto. Una vez que los niños dominan el texto y el contenido, el libro puede ser leído de manera independiente. ¡Estos libros les resultarán útiles, estimulantes y divertidos a niños y a adultos por igual!

— Susan Nations, M.Ed., autora/tutora de alfabetización/
consultora de desarrollo de la lectura

Did you ever see a bird with a **bill**, or beak, as long as this one? This bird is a **pelican** (PEL-ih-kan).

¿Has visto alguna vez un pájaro con un **pico** tan largo como éste? Este pájaro es un **pelícano**.

bill/
pico

Pelicans live near water in places all over the world. The map shows some places in North America and South America where pelicans build their **nests**.

Los pelícanos viven por todo el mundo, en lugares cercanos al agua. Este mapa muestra algunos lugares de América del Norte y del Sur donde los pelícanos hacen sus **nidos**.

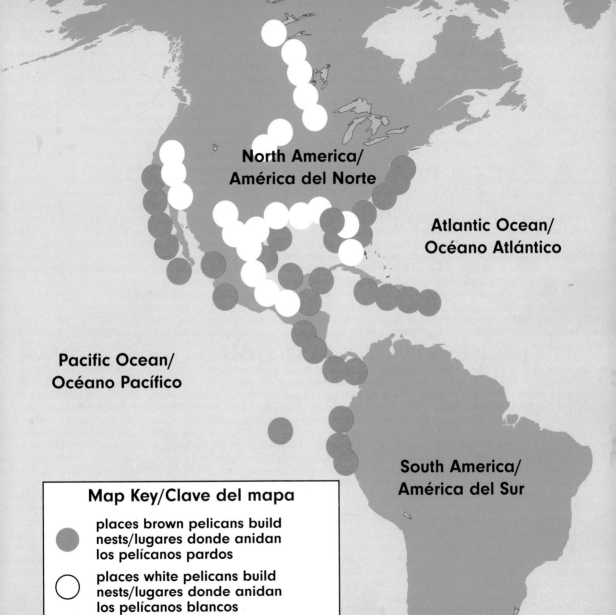

North America/
América del Norte

Atlantic Ocean/
Océano Atlántico

Pacific Ocean/
Océano Pacífico

South America/
América del Sur

Map Key/Clave del mapa

places brown pelicans build
nests/lugares donde anidan
los pelícanos pardos

places white pelicans build
nests/lugares donde anidan
los pelícanos blancos

7

A pelican has a **pouch** under its bill. It uses the pouch to catch fish. The pouch stretches to hold lots of fish.

Un pelícano tiene una **bolsa** debajo del pico. El pelícano utiliza la bolsa para atrapar peces. La bolsa se estira y puede contener muchos peces.

pouch/
bolsa

To find fish, a brown pelican flies high above the ocean. When it sees some fish, the bird **dives**.

Cuando va en busca de peces, un pelícano pardo vuela a gran altura sobre el océano. Cuando ve alguno, se **lanza en picado**.

A brown pelican dives into the water headfirst! It scoops fish into its pouch.

¡Un pelícano pardo se lanza al agua de cabeza! Usa la bolsa como un cucharón para atrapar peces.

13

White pelicans fish in groups. They herd fish into shallow water to catch them.

Los pelícanos blancos pescan en grupo. Para atrapar peces, los acorralan en aguas poco profundas.

Pelicans do not chew their food. They swallow it whole!

Los pelícanos no mastican la comida. ¡Se la tragan entera!

A hungry baby pelican cannot swallow a whole fish. It sticks its bill into its parent's pouch to eat soft pieces of fish.

Una cría de pelícano hambrienta no puede tragarse un pez entero. Mete el pico en la bolsa de uno de sus padres para comer pedazos blandos de pescado.

Pelicans are fun to watch! Look for them when you are near the ocean.

¡Es divertido ver a los pelícanos! Búscalos la próxima vez que estés cerca del océano.

Glossary/Glosario

bill — the hard outer part of a bird's mouth, also called a beak

dives — drops headfirst from a high place toward water

herd — to gather or force into a group by chasing

nests — places where mother birds or other female animals lay their eggs

pouch — the baglike part of a pelican's bill

stretches — becomes larger when pulled or pushed outward

---

acorralar — perseguir o rodear animales para obligarlos a agruparse

bolsa — parte del cuerpo de un pelícano situada bajo el pico

estirarse — hacerse más grande una cosa cuando se tira de ella

lanzarse en picado — arrojarse al agua de cabeza desde gran altura

nidos — lugares donde las hembras de aves y de otros animales depositan sus huevos

pico — parte dura externa de la boca de las aves

For More Information/Más información

Books

The Adventures of Pelican Pete: A Bird Is Born. Pelican Pete (series). Hugh and Frances Keiser (Sagaponack Books)

Flying Brown Pelicans. Anne Welsbacher (Lerner Publications)

The Proud Pelican's Secret. Animal Storybooks (series). Rebecca Johnson (Gareth Stevens)

Seeing Seabirds. Rookie Read-About Science (series). Allan Fowler (Children's Press)

Libros

Pelícanos. Aves (series). Lynn M. Stone (Rourke Publishing)

Las aventuras de Pedro Pelícano: un ave nace. Hugh and Frances Keiser (Sagaponack Books)

Index/Índice

baby pelicans 18
bills 4, 5, 8, 18
brown pelicans 7, 10, 12
diving 10, 12
fish 8, 10, 12, 14, 18
flying 10
food 16
nests 6, 7
oceans 10, 20
pouches 8, 9, 12, 18
water 6, 12, 14
white pelicans 7, 14

agua 6, 12, 14
bolsas 8, 9, 12, 18
comida 16
crías de pelícano 18
lanzarse en picado 10, 12
nidos 6, 7
océanos 10, 20
peces 8, 10, 12, 14, 18
pelícanos blancos 7, 14
pelícanos pardos 7, 10, 12
picos 4, 5, 8, 18
volar 10

About the Author/Información sobre la autora

Kathleen Pohl has written and edited many children's books. Among them are animal tales, rhyming books, retold classics, and the forty-book series *Nature Close-Ups*. She and her husband, Bruce, live in the middle of beautiful Wisconsin woods and share their home with six goats, a llama, and all kinds of wonderful woodland creatures.

Kathleen Pohl ha escrito y corregido muchos libros infantiles. Entre ellos hay cuentos de animales, libros de rimas, versiones nuevas de cuentos clásicos y la serie de cuarenta libros *Nature Close-Ups*. Kathleen vive con su marido, Bruce, en medio de los bellos bosques de Wisconsin. Ambos comparten su hogar con seis cabras, una llama y todo tipo de maravillosos animales del bosque.